COCKTAIL RECIPE BOOK

TO WRITE IN YOUR OWN RECIPES

THIS BOOK BELONGS TO

_____

PHONE: ....

EMAIL: ....

START DATE: ....

END DATE: ....

Index

COCKTAIL NAME

#	COCKTAIL NAME	RATING
1		☆☆☆☆☆
2		☆☆☆☆☆
3		☆☆☆☆☆
4		☆☆☆☆☆
5		☆☆☆☆☆
6		☆☆☆☆☆
7		☆☆☆☆☆
8		☆☆☆☆☆
9		☆☆☆☆☆
10		☆☆☆☆☆
11		☆☆☆☆☆
12		☆☆☆☆☆
13		☆☆☆☆☆
14		☆☆☆☆☆
15		☆☆☆☆☆
16		☆☆☆☆☆
17		☆☆☆☆☆
18		☆☆☆☆☆
19		☆☆☆☆☆
20		☆☆☆☆☆
21		☆☆☆☆☆
22		☆☆☆☆☆
23		☆☆☆☆☆
24		☆☆☆☆☆
25		☆☆☆☆☆

Index

#	COCKTAIL NAME	RATING
26		☆☆☆☆☆
27		☆☆☆☆☆
28		☆☆☆☆☆
29		☆☆☆☆☆
30		☆☆☆☆☆
31		☆☆☆☆☆
32		☆☆☆☆☆
33		☆☆☆☆☆
34		☆☆☆☆☆
35		☆☆☆☆☆
36		☆☆☆☆☆
37		☆☆☆☆☆
38		☆☆☆☆☆
39		☆☆☆☆☆
40		☆☆☆☆☆
41		☆☆☆☆☆
42		☆☆☆☆☆
43		☆☆☆☆☆
44		☆☆☆☆☆
45		☆☆☆☆☆
46		☆☆☆☆☆
47		☆☆☆☆☆
48		☆☆☆☆☆
49		☆☆☆☆☆
50		☆☆☆☆☆

Index

#	COCKTAIL NAME	RATING
51		☆☆☆☆☆
52		☆☆☆☆☆
53		☆☆☆☆☆
53		☆☆☆☆☆
55		☆☆☆☆☆
56		☆☆☆☆☆
57		☆☆☆☆☆
58		☆☆☆☆☆
59		☆☆☆☆☆
60		☆☆☆☆☆
61		☆☆☆☆☆
62		☆☆☆☆☆
63		☆☆☆☆☆
64		☆☆☆☆☆
65		☆☆☆☆☆
66		☆☆☆☆☆
67		☆☆☆☆☆
68		☆☆☆☆☆
69		☆☆☆☆☆
70		☆☆☆☆☆
71		☆☆☆☆☆
72		☆☆☆☆☆
73		☆☆☆☆☆
74		☆☆☆☆☆
75		☆☆☆☆☆

Index

#	COCKTAIL NAME	RATING
76		☆☆☆☆☆
77		☆☆☆☆☆
78		☆☆☆☆☆
79		☆☆☆☆☆
80		☆☆☆☆☆
81		☆☆☆☆☆
82		☆☆☆☆☆
83		☆☆☆☆☆
84		☆☆☆☆☆
85		☆☆☆☆☆
86		☆☆☆☆☆
87		☆☆☆☆☆
88		☆☆☆☆☆
89		☆☆☆☆☆
90		☆☆☆☆☆
91		☆☆☆☆☆
92		☆☆☆☆☆
93		☆☆☆☆☆
94		☆☆☆☆☆
95		☆☆☆☆☆
96		☆☆☆☆☆
97		☆☆☆☆☆
98		☆☆☆☆☆
99		☆☆☆☆☆
100		☆☆☆☆☆

꿀 NAME _____   📅 DATE _____

☐ ☐ ☐ ☐ ☐ ☐ ☐ ☐ ☐ ☐

INGREDIENTS

_____ _____   _____ _____

_____ _____   _____ _____

_____ _____   _____ _____

_____ _____   _____ _____

GARNISH

_____   _____

_____   _____

_____   _____

INSTRUCTIONS

_____

_____

_____

_____

_____

_____

DIFFICULTY ⭕⭕⭕⭕⭕   OVERALL RATING ☆☆☆☆☆

NAME _____   DATE _____

GLASS TYPE

☐ ☐ ☐ ☐ ☐ ☐ ☐ ☐ ☐ ☐

INGREDIENTS

_____ _____   _____ _____

_____ _____   _____ _____

_____ _____   _____ _____

_____ _____   _____ _____

GARNISH

_____   _____

_____   _____

_____   _____

INSTRUCTIONS

_____

_____

_____

_____

_____

DIFFICULTY ⭘⭘⭘⭘⭘   OVERALL RATING ☆☆☆☆☆

🍸 NAME _____   📅 DATE _____

GLASS TYPE

☐ ☐ ☐ ☐ ☐ ☐ ☐ ☐ ☐ ☐

INGREDIENTS

___ _____   ___ _____

___ _____   ___ _____

___ _____   ___ _____

GARNISH

_____   _____

_____   _____

_____   _____

INSTRUCTIONS

_____

_____

_____

_____

_____

DIFFICULTY ⚪⚪⚪⚪⚪   OVERALL RATING ☆☆☆☆☆

🍸 NAME _____   📅 DATE _____

GLASS TYPE

☐ ☐ ☐ ☐ ☐ ☐ ☐ ☐ ☐ ☐

INGREDIENTS

_____ _____   _____ _____

_____ _____   _____ _____

_____ _____   _____ _____

_____ _____   _____ _____

GARNISH

_____ _____

_____ _____

_____ _____

INSTRUCTIONS

_____

_____

_____

_____

_____

DIFFICULTY ⭘⭘⭘⭘⭘   OVERALL RATING ☆☆☆☆☆

4

NAME _____ DATE _____

GLASS TYPE

☐ ☐ ☐ ☐ ☐ ☐ ☐ ☐ ☐ ☐

INGREDIENTS

_____ _____ _____ _____

_____ _____ _____ _____

_____ _____ _____ _____

_____ _____ _____ _____

GARNISH

_____ _____

_____ _____

_____ _____

INSTRUCTIONS

_____

_____

_____

_____

_____

_____

DIFFICULTY ○○○○○   OVERALL RATING ☆☆☆☆☆

🍸 NAME _____ 📅 DATE _____

GLASS TYPE

☐ ☐ ☐ ☐ ☐ ☐ ☐ ☐ ☐ ☐

INGREDIENTS

_____ _____   _____ _____

_____ _____   _____ _____

_____ _____   _____ _____

_____ _____   _____ _____

GARNISH

_____ _____   _____

_____ _____   _____

_____ _____   _____

INSTRUCTIONS

_____

_____

_____

_____

_____

DIFFICULTY ○○○○○   **OVERALL RATING** ☆☆☆☆☆

GLASS TYPE

☐ ☐ ☐ ☐ ☐ ☐ ☐ ☐ ☐ ☐

INGREDIENTS

_____ _____   _____ _____

_____ _____   _____ _____

_____ _____   _____ _____

_____ _____   _____ _____

GARNISH

_____   _____

_____   _____

_____   _____

INSTRUCTIONS

_____

_____

_____

_____

_____

_____

_____

DIFFICULTY ○○○○○　　OVERALL RATING ☆☆☆☆☆

GLASS TYPE

☐ ☐ ☐ ☐ ☐ ☐ ☐ ☐ ☐ ☐

INGREDIENTS

_____ _____   _____ _____

_____ _____   _____ _____

_____ _____   _____ _____

_____ _____   _____ _____

GARNISH

_____   _____

_____   _____

_____   _____

INSTRUCTIONS

_____

_____

_____

_____

_____

_____

DIFFICULTY ○○○○○   **OVERALL RATING** ☆☆☆☆☆

GLASS TYPE

☐ ☐ ☐ ☐ ☐ ☐ ☐ ☐ ☐ ☐

INGREDIENTS

_____ _____   _____ _____

_____ _____   _____ _____

_____ _____   _____ _____

_____ _____   _____ _____

GARNISH

_____   _____

_____   _____

_____   _____

INSTRUCTIONS

_____

_____

_____

_____

_____

_____

DIFFICULTY ⭕⭕⭕⭕⭕   OVERALL RATING ☆☆☆☆☆

🍸 NAME _____   📅 DATE _____

☐ ☐ ☐ ☐ ☐ ☐ ☐ ☐ ☐ ☐

INGREDIENTS

_____ _____   _____ _____

_____ _____   _____ _____

_____ _____   _____ _____

_____ _____   _____ _____

GARNISH

_____ _____   _____ _____

_____ _____   _____ _____

_____ _____   _____ _____

INSTRUCTIONS

_____

_____

_____

_____

_____

DIFFICULTY ○○○○○   OVERALL RATING ☆☆☆☆☆

🍸 NAME _____   📅 DATE _____

GLASS TYPE

☐ ☐ ☐ ☐ ☐ ☐ ☐ ☐ ☐ ☐

INGREDIENTS

_____ _____   _____ _____
_____ _____   _____ _____
_____ _____   _____ _____
_____ _____   _____ _____

GARNISH

_____   _____
_____   _____
_____   _____

INSTRUCTIONS

_____
_____
_____
_____
_____
_____

DIFFICULTY ○○○○○   OVERALL RATING ☆☆☆☆☆

NAME _____ DATE _____

GLASS TYPE

☐ ☐ ☐ ☐ ☐ ☐ ☐ ☐ ☐ ☐

INGREDIENTS

_____ _____   _____ _____

_____ _____   _____ _____

_____ _____   _____ _____

_____ _____   _____ _____

GARNISH

_____ _____   _____ _____

_____ _____   _____ _____

_____ _____   _____ _____

INSTRUCTIONS

_____

_____

_____

_____

_____

_____

DIFFICULTY ○○○○○   OVERALL RATING ☆☆☆☆☆

GLASS TYPE

☐ ☐ ☐ ☐ ☐ ☐ ☐ ☐ ☐ ☐

INGREDIENTS

_____ _____   _____ _____

_____ _____   _____ _____

_____ _____   _____ _____

_____ _____   _____ _____

GARNISH

_____   _____

_____   _____

_____   _____

INSTRUCTIONS

_____

_____

_____

_____

_____

_____

DIFFICULTY ○○○○○   OVERALL RATING ☆☆☆☆☆

NAME _____   DATE _____

GLASS TYPE

☐ ☐ ☐ ☐ ☐ ☐ ☐ ☐ ☐ ☐

INGREDIENTS

_____ _____   _____ _____

_____ _____   _____ _____

_____ _____   _____ _____

_____ _____   _____ _____

GARNISH

_____   _____

_____   _____

_____   _____

INSTRUCTIONS

_____

_____

_____

_____

_____

DIFFICULTY ○○○○○   OVERALL RATING ☆☆☆☆☆

GLASS TYPE

☐ ☐ ☐ ☐ ☐ ☐ ☐ ☐ ☐ ☐

INGREDIENTS

_____ _____ _____ _____

_____ _____ _____ _____

_____ _____ _____ _____

_____ _____ _____ _____

GARNISH

_____ _____

_____ _____

_____ _____

INSTRUCTIONS

_____

_____

_____

_____

_____

_____

DIFFICULTY ○○○○○   **OVERALL RATING** ☆☆☆☆☆

NAME _____   DATE _____

GLASS TYPE

☐ ☐ ☐ ☐ ☐ ☐ ☐ ☐ ☐ ☐

INGREDIENTS

_____ _____ _____ _____

_____ _____ _____ _____

_____ _____ _____ _____

_____ _____ _____ _____

GARNISH

_____ _____

_____ _____

_____ _____

INSTRUCTIONS

_____

_____

_____

_____

_____

_____

DIFFICULTY ○○○○○   OVERALL RATING ☆☆☆☆☆

🍸 NAME _____   📅 DATE _____

GLASS TYPE

☐ ☐ ☐ ☐ ☐ ☐ ☐ ☐ ☐ ☐

INGREDIENTS

_____ _____   _____ _____

_____ _____   _____ _____

_____ _____   _____ _____

_____ _____   _____ _____

GARNISH

_____   _____

_____   _____

_____   _____

INSTRUCTIONS

_____

_____

_____

_____

_____

_____

DIFFICULTY ○○○○○   OVERALL RATING ☆☆☆☆☆

NAME _____   DATE _____

GLASS TYPE

☐ ☐ ☐ ☐ ☐ ☐ ☐ ☐ ☐ ☐

INGREDIENTS

_____ _____   _____ _____

_____ _____   _____ _____

_____ _____   _____ _____

_____ _____   _____ _____

GARNISH

_____   _____

_____   _____

_____   _____

INSTRUCTIONS

_____

_____

_____

_____

_____

DIFFICULTY ○○○○○   OVERALL RATING ☆☆☆☆☆

GLASS TYPE

☐ ☐ ☐ ☐ ☐ ☐ ☐ ☐ ☐ ☐

INGREDIENTS

_____ _____   _____ _____

_____ _____   _____ _____

_____ _____   _____ _____

_____ _____   _____ _____

GARNISH

_____   _____

_____   _____

_____   _____

INSTRUCTIONS

_____

_____

_____

_____

_____

_____

DIFFICULTY ○○○○○   OVERALL RATING ☆☆☆☆☆

NAME _____   DATE _____

GLASS TYPE

☐ ☐ ☐ ☐ ☐ ☐ ☐ ☐ ☐ ☐

INGREDIENTS

_____ _____   _____ _____

_____ _____   _____ _____

_____ _____   _____ _____

_____ _____   _____ _____

GARNISH

_____   _____

_____   _____

_____   _____

INSTRUCTIONS

_____

_____

_____

_____

_____

DIFFICULTY ○○○○○   OVERALL RATING ☆☆☆☆☆

GLASS TYPE

☐ ☐ ☐ ☐ ☐ ☐ ☐ ☐ ☐ ☐

INGREDIENTS

_____ _____   _____ _____
_____ _____   _____ _____
_____ _____   _____ _____
_____ _____   _____ _____

GARNISH

_____   _____
_____   _____
_____   _____

INSTRUCTIONS

_____
_____
_____
_____
_____
_____

DIFFICULTY ⃝⃝⃝⃝⃝   OVERALL RATING ☆☆☆☆☆

NAME _____   DATE _____

GLASS TYPE

☐ ☐ ☐ ☐ ☐ ☐ ☐ ☐ ☐ ☐

INGREDIENTS

_____ _____   _____ _____

_____ _____   _____ _____

_____ _____   _____ _____

_____ _____   _____ _____

GARNISH

_____   _____

_____   _____

_____   _____

INSTRUCTIONS

_____

_____

_____

_____

_____

DIFFICULTY ○○○○○   OVERALL RATING ☆☆☆☆☆

GLASS TYPE

☐ ☐ ☐ ☐ ☐ ☐ ☐ ☐ ☐ ☐

INGREDIENTS

_____ _____   _____ _____

_____ _____   _____ _____

_____ _____   _____ _____

_____ _____   _____ _____

GARNISH

_____   _____

_____   _____

_____   _____

INSTRUCTIONS

_____

_____

_____

_____

_____

_____

DIFFICULTY ○○○○○   OVERALL RATING ☆☆☆☆☆

NAME _____   DATE _____

GLASS TYPE

☐ ☐ ☐ ☐ ☐ ☐ ☐ ☐ ☐ ☐

INGREDIENTS

_____ _____   _____ _____

_____ _____   _____ _____

_____ _____   _____ _____

_____ _____   _____ _____

GARNISH

_____   _____

_____   _____

_____   _____

INSTRUCTIONS

_____

_____

_____

_____

_____

_____

DIFFICULTY ○○○○○   OVERALL RATING ☆☆☆☆☆

GLASS TYPE

☐ ☐ ☐ ☐ ☐ ☐ ☐ ☐ ☐ ☐

INGREDIENTS

_____ _____   _____ _____

_____ _____   _____ _____

_____ _____   _____ _____

_____ _____   _____ _____

GARNISH

_____ _____   _____ _____

_____ _____   _____ _____

_____ _____   _____ _____

INSTRUCTIONS

_____

_____

_____

_____

_____

_____

DIFFICULTY ⭕⭕⭕⭕⭕   OVERALL RATING ☆☆☆☆☆

🍸 NAME _____　　📅 DATE _____

GLASS TYPE

☐　☐　☐　☐　☐　☐　☐　☐　☐　☐

INGREDIENTS

_____　_____　_____　_____

_____　_____　_____　_____

_____　_____　_____　_____

_____　_____　_____　_____

GARNISH

_____　_____

_____　_____

_____　_____

INSTRUCTIONS

_____

_____

_____

_____

_____

_____

DIFFICULTY ⭕⭕⭕⭕⭕　　OVERALL RATING ☆☆☆☆☆

GLASS TYPE

☐ ☐ ☐ ☐ ☐ ☐ ☐ ☐ ☐ ☐

INGREDIENTS

_____ _____   _____ _____

_____ _____   _____ _____

_____ _____   _____ _____

_____ _____   _____ _____

GARNISH

_____   _____

_____   _____

_____   _____

INSTRUCTIONS

_____

_____

_____

_____

_____

_____

DIFFICULTY ○○○○○   OVERALL RATING ☆☆☆☆☆

GLASS TYPE

☐ ☐ ☐ ☐ ☐ ☐ ☐ ☐ ☐ ☐

INGREDIENTS

_____ _____ _____ _____

_____ _____ _____ _____

_____ _____ _____ _____

_____ _____ _____ _____

GARNISH

_____ _____

_____ _____

_____ _____

INSTRUCTIONS

_____

_____

_____

_____

_____

DIFFICULTY ○○○○○   OVERALL RATING ☆☆☆☆☆

GLASS TYPE

☐ ☐ ☐ ☐ ☐ ☐ ☐ ☐ ☐ ☐

INGREDIENTS

_____ _____   _____ _____

_____ _____   _____ _____

_____ _____   _____ _____

_____ _____   _____ _____

GARNISH

_____ _____

_____ _____

_____ _____

INSTRUCTIONS

_____

_____

_____

_____

_____

_____

DIFFICULTY ○○○○○   OVERALL RATING ☆☆☆☆☆

🍸 NAME _____   📅 DATE _____

GLASS TYPE

☐   ☐   ☐   ☐   ☐   ☐   ☐   ☐   ☐   ☐

INGREDIENTS

_____ _____   _____ _____

_____ _____   _____ _____

_____ _____   _____ _____

_____ _____   _____ _____

GARNISH

_____   _____

_____   _____

_____   _____

INSTRUCTIONS

_____

_____

_____

_____

_____

_____

DIFFICULTY ○○○○○   OVERALL RATING ☆☆☆☆☆

GLASS TYPE

☐ ☐ ☐ ☐ ☐ ☐ ☐ ☐ ☐ ☐

INGREDIENTS

_____ _____   _____ _____

_____ _____   _____ _____

_____ _____   _____ _____

_____ _____   _____ _____

GARNISH

_____   _____

_____   _____

_____   _____

INSTRUCTIONS

_____

_____

_____

_____

_____

_____

DIFFICULTY ○○○○○   OVERALL RATING ☆☆☆☆☆

Y NAME _____   📅 DATE _____

GLASS TYPE

☐ ☐ ☐ ☐ ☐ ☐ ☐ ☐ ☐ ☐

INGREDIENTS

_____ _____   _____ _____

_____ _____   _____ _____

_____ _____   _____ _____

_____ _____

GARNISH

_____   _____

_____   _____

_____

INSTRUCTIONS

_____

_____

_____

_____

_____

DIFFICULTY ⭕⭕⭕⭕⭕   OVERALL RATING ☆☆☆☆☆

GLASS TYPE

☐ ☐ ☐ ☐ ☐ ☐ ☐ ☐ ☐ ☐

INGREDIENTS

_____ _____   _____

_____ _____   _____

_____ _____   _____

_____ _____   _____

GARNISH

_____   _____

_____   _____

_____   _____

INSTRUCTIONS

_____

_____

_____

_____

_____

DIFFICULTY ○○○○○   OVERALL RATING ☆☆☆☆☆

NAME _____ DATE _____

GLASS TYPE

☐ ☐ ☐ ☐ ☐ ☐ ☐ ☐ ☐ ☐

INGREDIENTS

_____ _____   _____ _____

_____ _____   _____ _____

_____ _____   _____ _____

_____ _____

GARNISH

_____   _____

_____   _____

_____   _____

INSTRUCTIONS

_____

_____

_____

_____

_____

DIFFICULTY ○○○○○   OVERALL RATING ☆☆☆☆☆

🍸 NAME _____   📅 DATE _____

🍶 **GLASS TYPE**

☐ ☐ ☐ ☐ ☐ ☐ ☐ ☐ ☐ ☐

🍋 **INGREDIENTS**

_____ _____   _____ _____

_____ _____   _____ _____

_____ _____   _____ _____

_____ _____   _____ _____

🌿 **GARNISH**

_____   _____

_____   _____

_____   _____

🍸 **INSTRUCTIONS**

_____

_____

_____

_____

_____

_____

DIFFICULTY ○○○○○   OVERALL RATING ☆☆☆☆☆

NAME _____ DATE _____

GLASS TYPE

☐ ☐ ☐ ☐ ☐ ☐ ☐ ☐ ☐ ☐

INGREDIENTS

_____ _____   _____ _____

_____ _____   _____ _____

_____ _____   _____ _____

_____ _____   _____ _____

GARNISH

_____   _____

_____   _____

_____   _____

INSTRUCTIONS

_____

_____

_____

_____

_____

DIFFICULTY ○○○○○   OVERALL RATING ☆☆☆☆☆

🍸 NAME _____   📅 DATE _____

GLASS TYPE

☐ ☐ ☐ ☐ ☐ ☐ ☐ ☐ ☐ ☐

INGREDIENTS

_____ _____   _____ _____

_____ _____   _____ _____

_____ _____   _____ _____

_____ _____   _____ _____

GARNISH

_____   _____

_____   _____

_____   _____

INSTRUCTIONS

_____

_____

_____

_____

_____

_____

DIFFICULTY ⭕⭕⭕⭕⭕   OVERALL RATING ☆☆☆☆☆

GLASS TYPE

☐ ☐ ☐ ☐ ☐ ☐ ☐ ☐ ☐ ☐

INGREDIENTS

_____ _____   _____ _____

_____ _____   _____ _____

_____ _____   _____ _____

_____ _____   _____ _____

GARNISH

_____   _____

_____   _____

_____   _____

INSTRUCTIONS

_____

_____

_____

_____

_____

_____

DIFFICULTY ○○○○○   OVERALL RATING ☆☆☆☆☆

GLASS TYPE

☐ ☐ ☐ ☐ ☐ ☐ ☐ ☐ ☐ ☐

INGREDIENTS

_____ _____ _____ _____

_____ _____ _____ _____

_____ _____ _____ _____

_____ _____ _____ _____

GARNISH

_____ _____

_____ _____

_____ _____

INSTRUCTIONS

_____

_____

_____

_____

_____

_____

DIFFICULTY ○○○○○   OVERALL RATING ☆☆☆☆☆

🍸 NAME _____   📅 DATE _____

GLASS TYPE

☐ ☐ ☐ ☐ ☐ ☐ ☐ ☐ ☐ ☐

INGREDIENTS

_____ _____   _____ _____

_____ _____   _____ _____

_____ _____   _____ _____

_____ _____   _____ _____

GARNISH

_____   _____

_____   _____

_____   _____

INSTRUCTIONS

_____

_____

_____

_____

_____

DIFFICULTY ⃝⃝⃝⃝⃝   OVERALL RATING ☆☆☆☆☆

🍸 NAME _____   📅 DATE _____

GLASS TYPE

☐ ☐ ☐ ☐ ☐ ☐ ☐ ☐ ☐ ☐

INGREDIENTS

_____ _____   _____ _____

_____ _____   _____ _____

_____ _____   _____ _____

_____ _____   _____ _____

GARNISH

_____ _____

_____ _____

_____ _____

INSTRUCTIONS

_____

_____

_____

_____

_____

_____

DIFFICULTY ○○○○○   **OVERALL RATING** ☆☆☆☆☆

🍸 NAME _____   📅 DATE _____

GLASS TYPE

☐ ☐ ☐ ☐ ☐ ☐ ☐ ☐ ☐ ☐

INGREDIENTS

_____ _____   _____ _____

_____ _____   _____ _____

_____ _____   _____ _____

_____ _____   _____ _____

GARNISH

_____   _____

_____   _____

_____   _____

INSTRUCTIONS

_____

_____

_____

_____

_____

_____

DIFFICULTY ○○○○○   OVERALL RATING ☆☆☆☆☆

NAME _____   DATE _____

GLASS TYPE

☐ ☐ ☐ ☐ ☐ ☐ ☐ ☐ ☐ ☐

INGREDIENTS

_____ _____   _____ _____

_____ _____   _____ _____

_____ _____   _____ _____

_____ _____   _____ _____

GARNISH

_____ _____   _____ _____

_____ _____   _____ _____

_____ _____   _____ _____

INSTRUCTIONS

_____

_____

_____

_____

_____

DIFFICULTY ○○○○○   OVERALL RATING ☆☆☆☆☆

GLASS TYPE

☐ ☐ ☐ ☐ ☐ ☐ ☐ ☐ ☐ ☐

INGREDIENTS

_____ _____   _____ _____

_____ _____   _____ _____

_____ _____   _____ _____

_____ _____

GARNISH

_____   _____

_____   _____

_____   _____

INSTRUCTIONS

_____

_____

_____

_____

_____

_____

DIFFICULTY ○○○○○   OVERALL RATING ☆☆☆☆☆

GLASS TYPE

☐ ☐ ☐ ☐ ☐ ☐ ☐ ☐ ☐ ☐

INGREDIENTS

_____ _____   _____ _____

_____ _____   _____ _____

_____ _____   _____ _____

_____ _____   _____ _____

GARNISH

_____   _____

_____   _____

_____   _____

INSTRUCTIONS

_____

_____

_____

_____

_____

_____

DIFFICULTY ○○○○○   OVERALL RATING ☆☆☆☆☆

🍸 NAME _____   📅 DATE _____

🧴 **GLASS TYPE**

☐ ☐ ☐ ☐ ☐ ☐ ☐ ☐ ☐ ☐

🍋 **INGREDIENTS**

_____ _____   _____ _____

_____ _____   _____ _____

_____ _____   _____ _____

_____ _____   _____ _____

🌿 **GARNISH**

_____   _____

_____   _____

_____   _____

🍸 **INSTRUCTIONS**

_____

_____

_____

_____

_____

DIFFICULTY ○○○○○   OVERALL RATING ☆☆☆☆☆

GLASS TYPE

☐ ☐ ☐ ☐ ☐ ☐ ☐ ☐ ☐ ☐

INGREDIENTS

_____ _____

_____ _____

_____ _____

_____ _____

GARNISH

_____ _____

_____ _____

_____ _____

INSTRUCTIONS

_____

_____

_____

_____

_____

_____

DIFFICULTY ○○○○○   OVERALL RATING ☆☆☆☆☆

GLASS TYPE

☐ ☐ ☐ ☐ ☐ ☐ ☐ ☐ ☐ ☐

INGREDIENTS

_____ _____   _____ _____

_____ _____   _____ _____

_____ _____   _____ _____

_____ _____   _____ _____

GARNISH

_____   _____

_____   _____

_____   _____

INSTRUCTIONS

_____

_____

_____

_____

_____

_____

DIFFICULTY ○○○○○   OVERALL RATING ☆☆☆☆☆

🍸 NAME _____   📅 DATE _____

🧃
GLASS TYPE

☐ ☐ ☐ ☐ ☐ ☐ ☐ ☐ ☐ ☐

🍋
INGREDIENTS

_____ _____   _____ _____

_____ _____   _____ _____

_____ _____   _____ _____

🌿
GARNISH

_____   _____

_____   _____

_____   _____

🍸
INSTRUCTIONS

_____

_____

_____

_____

_____

DIFFICULTY ○○○○○   OVERALL RATING ☆☆☆☆☆

GLASS TYPE

☐ ☐ ☐ ☐ ☐ ☐ ☐ ☐ ☐ ☐

INGREDIENTS

_____ _____   _____ _____

_____ _____   _____ _____

_____ _____   _____ _____

_____ _____   _____ _____

GARNISH

_____   _____

_____   _____

_____   _____

INSTRUCTIONS

_____

_____

_____

_____

_____

DIFFICULTY ○○○○○   OVERALL RATING ☆☆☆☆☆

GLASS TYPE

☐ ☐ ☐ ☐ ☐ ☐ ☐ ☐ ☐ ☐

INGREDIENTS

_____ _____ _____ _____

_____ _____ _____ _____

_____ _____ _____ _____

_____ _____ _____ _____

GARNISH

_____ _____

_____ _____

_____ _____

INSTRUCTIONS

_____

_____

_____

_____

_____

DIFFICULTY ○○○○○   OVERALL RATING ☆☆☆☆☆

🍸 NAME _____ 📅 DATE _____

GLASS TYPE

☐ ☐ ☐ ☐ ☐ ☐ ☐ ☐ ☐ ☐

INGREDIENTS

_____ _____ _____ _____

_____ _____ _____ _____

_____ _____ _____ _____

_____ _____ _____ _____

GARNISH

_____ _____

_____ _____

_____ _____

INSTRUCTIONS

_____

_____

_____

_____

_____

DIFFICULTY ○○○○○   OVERALL RATING ☆☆☆☆☆

🍸 NAME _____   📅 DATE _____

☐ ☐ ☐ ☐ ☐ ☐ ☐ ☐ ☐ ☐

INGREDIENTS

_____ _____   _____ _____

_____ _____   _____ _____

_____ _____   _____ _____

_____ _____   _____ _____

GARNISH

_____ _____

_____ _____

_____ _____

INSTRUCTIONS

_____

_____

_____

_____

_____

_____

DIFFICULTY ○○○○○   OVERALL RATING ☆☆☆☆☆

🍸 NAME _____   📅 DATE _____

GLASS TYPE

☐ ☐ ☐ ☐ ☐ ☐ ☐ ☐ ☐ ☐

INGREDIENTS

_____ _____ _____ _____

_____ _____ _____ _____

_____ _____ _____ _____

_____ _____ _____ _____

GARNISH

_____ _____

_____ _____

_____ _____

INSTRUCTIONS

_____

_____

_____

_____

_____

DIFFICULTY ○○○○○   OVERALL RATING ☆☆☆☆☆

GLASS TYPE

☐ ☐ ☐ ☐ ☐ ☐ ☐ ☐ ☐ ☐

INGREDIENTS

_____ _____ _____ _____

_____ _____ _____ _____

_____ _____ _____ _____

_____ _____ _____ _____

GARNISH

_____ _____

_____ _____

_____ _____

INSTRUCTIONS

_____

_____

_____

_____

_____

_____

DIFFICULTY ⭕⭕⭕⭕⭕   OVERALL RATING ☆☆☆☆☆

GLASS TYPE

☐ ☐ ☐ ☐ ☐ ☐ ☐ ☐ ☐ ☐

INGREDIENTS

_____ _____ _____ _____

_____ _____ _____ _____

_____ _____ _____ _____

_____ _____ _____ _____

GARNISH

_____ _____

_____ _____

_____ _____

INSTRUCTIONS

_____

_____

_____

_____

_____

_____

DIFFICULTY ○○○○○   OVERALL RATING ☆☆☆☆☆

NAME _____ DATE _____

GLASS TYPE

☐ ☐ ☐ ☐ ☐ ☐ ☐ ☐ ☐ ☐

INGREDIENTS

_____ _____   _____ _____

_____ _____   _____ _____

_____ _____   _____ _____

_____ _____   _____ _____

GARNISH

_____   _____

_____   _____

_____   _____

INSTRUCTIONS

_____

_____

_____

_____

_____

DIFFICULTY ○○○○○   OVERALL RATING ☆☆☆☆☆

GLASS TYPE

☐ ☐ ☐ ☐ ☐ ☐ ☐ ☐ ☐ ☐

INGREDIENTS

_____ _____ _____ _____

_____ _____ _____ _____

_____ _____ _____ _____

_____ _____ _____ _____

GARNISH

_____ _____

_____ _____

_____ _____

INSTRUCTIONS

_____

_____

_____

_____

_____

DIFFICULTY ○○○○○   OVERALL RATING ☆☆☆☆☆

GLASS TYPE

☐ ☐ ☐ ☐ ☐ ☐ ☐ ☐ ☐ ☐

INGREDIENTS

_____ _____ _____ _____

_____ _____ _____ _____

_____ _____ _____ _____

_____ _____ _____ _____

GARNISH

_____ _____

_____ _____

_____ _____

INSTRUCTIONS

_____

_____

_____

_____

_____

DIFFICULTY ○○○○○   OVERALL RATING ☆☆☆☆☆

GLASS TYPE

☐ ☐ ☐ ☐ ☐ ☐ ☐ ☐ ☐ ☐

INGREDIENTS

_____ _____ _____ _____

_____ _____ _____ _____

_____ _____ _____ _____

_____ _____ _____ _____

GARNISH

_____ _____

_____ _____

_____ _____

_____ _____

INSTRUCTIONS

_____

_____

_____

_____

_____

_____

DIFFICULTY ○○○○○   OVERALL RATING ☆☆☆☆☆

NAME _____ DATE _____

GLASS TYPE

☐ ☐ ☐ ☐ ☐ ☐ ☐ ☐ ☐ ☐

INGREDIENTS

_____ _____   _____ _____

_____ _____   _____ _____

_____ _____   _____ _____

_____ _____   _____ _____

GARNISH

_____   _____

_____   _____

_____   _____

INSTRUCTIONS

_____

_____

_____

_____

_____

DIFFICULTY ○○○○○   OVERALL RATING ☆☆☆☆☆

GLASS TYPE

☐ ☐ ☐ ☐ ☐ ☐ ☐ ☐ ☐ ☐

INGREDIENTS

_____ _____   _____ _____

_____ _____   _____ _____

_____ _____   _____ _____

_____ _____   _____ _____

GARNISH

_____   _____

_____   _____

_____   _____

INSTRUCTIONS

_____

_____

_____

_____

_____

_____

DIFFICULTY ⭕⭕⭕⭕⭕   OVERALL RATING ☆☆☆☆☆

NAME _____   DATE _____

GLASS TYPE

☐ ☐ ☐ ☐ ☐ ☐ ☐ ☐ ☐ ☐

INGREDIENTS

_____ _____   _____ _____

_____ _____   _____ _____

_____ _____   _____ _____

_____ _____   _____ _____

GARNISH

_____   _____

_____   _____

_____   _____

INSTRUCTIONS

_____

_____

_____

_____

_____

DIFFICULTY ○○○○○   OVERALL RATING ☆☆☆☆☆

🍸 NAME _____   📅 DATE _____

GLASS TYPE

☐ ☐ ☐ ☐ ☐ ☐ ☐ ☐ ☐ ☐

INGREDIENTS

_____ _____   _____ _____

_____ _____   _____ _____

_____ _____   _____ _____

_____ _____   _____ _____

GARNISH

_____   _____

_____   _____

_____   _____

INSTRUCTIONS

_____

_____

_____

_____

_____

_____

DIFFICULTY ⭘⭘⭘⭘⭘   OVERALL RATING ☆☆☆☆☆

 NAME _____   DATE _____

GLASS TYPE

☐ ☐ ☐ ☐ ☐ ☐ ☐ ☐ ☐ ☐

INGREDIENTS

_____ _____   _____ _____

_____ _____   _____ _____

_____ _____   _____ _____

_____ _____   _____ _____

GARNISH

_____   _____

_____   _____

_____   _____

INSTRUCTIONS

_____

_____

_____

_____

_____

DIFFICULTY ○○○○○   OVERALL RATING ☆☆☆☆☆

GLASS TYPE

☐ ☐ ☐ ☐ ☐ ☐ ☐ ☐ ☐ ☐

INGREDIENTS

_____ _____ _____ _____
_____ _____ _____ _____
_____ _____ _____ _____
_____ _____ _____ _____

GARNISH

_____ _____
_____ _____
_____ _____

INSTRUCTIONS

_____
_____
_____
_____
_____
_____

DIFFICULTY ○○○○○   OVERALL RATING ☆☆☆☆☆

NAME _____   DATE _____

GLASS TYPE

☐ ☐ ☐ ☐ ☐ ☐ ☐ ☐ ☐ ☐

INGREDIENTS

_____ _____   _____ _____

_____ _____   _____ _____

_____ _____   _____ _____

_____ _____   _____ _____

GARNISH

_____   _____

_____   _____

_____   _____

INSTRUCTIONS

_____

_____

_____

_____

_____

DIFFICULTY ○○○○○   OVERALL RATING ☆☆☆☆☆

GLASS TYPE

☐ ☐ ☐ ☐ ☐ ☐ ☐ ☐ ☐ ☐

INGREDIENTS

_____ _____ _____ _____

_____ _____ _____ _____

_____ _____ _____ _____

_____ _____ _____ _____

GARNISH

_____ _____

_____ _____

_____ _____

INSTRUCTIONS

_____

_____

_____

_____

_____

_____

DIFFICULTY ○○○○○   OVERALL RATING ☆☆☆☆☆

GLASS TYPE

☐ ☐ ☐ ☐ ☐ ☐ ☐ ☐ ☐ ☐

INGREDIENTS

____ _____   _____ _____

____ _____   _____ _____

____ _____   _____ _____

____ _____   _____ _____

GARNISH

_____   _____

_____   _____

_____   _____

INSTRUCTIONS

_____

_____

_____

_____

_____

DIFFICULTY ○○○○○   **OVERALL RATING** ☆☆☆☆☆

🍸 NAME _____　　📅 DATE _____

☐ ☐ ☐ ☐ ☐ ☐ ☐ ☐ ☐ ☐

INGREDIENTS

_____　_____　　_____　_____

_____　_____　　_____　_____

_____　_____　　_____　_____

_____　_____　　_____　_____

GARNISH

_____　　_____

_____　　_____

_____　　_____

INSTRUCTIONS

_____

_____

_____

_____

_____

_____

DIFFICULTY ○○○○○　　OVERALL RATING ☆☆☆☆☆

GLASS TYPE

☐ ☐ ☐ ☐ ☐ ☐ ☐ ☐ ☐ ☐

INGREDIENTS

_____ _____   _____ _____

_____ _____   _____ _____

_____ _____   _____ _____

_____ _____   _____ _____

GARNISH

_____   _____

_____   _____

_____   _____

INSTRUCTIONS

_____

_____

_____

_____

_____

DIFFICULTY ⭕⭕⭕⭕⭕   OVERALL RATING ☆☆☆☆☆

🍸 NAME _____   📅 DATE _____

GLASS TYPE

☐ ☐ ☐ ☐ ☐ ☐ ☐ ☐ ☐ ☐

INGREDIENTS

_____ _____   _____ _____

_____ _____   _____ _____

_____ _____   _____ _____

_____ _____   _____ _____

GARNISH

_____   _____

_____   _____

_____   _____

INSTRUCTIONS

_____

_____

_____

_____

_____

_____

DIFFICULTY ○○○○○   OVERALL RATING ☆☆☆☆☆

🍸 NAME _____   📅 DATE _____

GLASS TYPE

☐ ☐ ☐ ☐ ☐ ☐ ☐ ☐ ☐ ☐

INGREDIENTS

_____ _____   _____ _____

_____ _____   _____ _____

_____ _____   _____ _____

_____ _____   _____ _____

GARNISH

_____   _____

_____   _____

_____   _____

INSTRUCTIONS

_____

_____

_____

_____

_____

DIFFICULTY ○○○○○   OVERALL RATING ☆☆☆☆☆

NAME _____ 📅 DATE _____

GLASS TYPE

☐ ☐ ☐ ☐ ☐ ☐ ☐ ☐ ☐ ☐

INGREDIENTS

_____ _____ _____ _____

_____ _____ _____ _____

_____ _____ _____ _____

_____ _____ _____ _____

GARNISH

_____ _____

_____ _____

_____ _____

INSTRUCTIONS

_____

_____

_____

_____

_____

_____

DIFFICULTY ○○○○○   OVERALL RATING ☆☆☆☆☆

74

GLASS TYPE

☐ ☐ ☐ ☐ ☐ ☐ ☐ ☐ ☐ ☐

INGREDIENTS

_____ _____   _____ _____

_____ _____   _____ _____

_____ _____   _____ _____

_____ _____   _____ _____

GARNISH

_____   _____

_____   _____

_____   _____

INSTRUCTIONS

_____

_____

_____

_____

_____

DIFFICULTY ○○○○○   OVERALL RATING ☆☆☆☆☆

🍸 NAME _____ 📅 DATE _____

GLASS TYPE

☐ ☐ ☐ ☐ ☐ ☐ ☐ ☐ ☐ ☐

INGREDIENTS

_____ _____ _____ _____

_____ _____ _____ _____

_____ _____ _____ _____

_____ _____ _____ _____

GARNISH

_____ _____

_____ _____

_____ _____

INSTRUCTIONS

_____

_____

_____

_____

_____

DIFFICULTY ⭕⭕⭕⭕⭕   OVERALL RATING ☆☆☆☆☆

Y NAME _____   📅 DATE _____

GLASS TYPE

☐ ☐ ☐ ☐ ☐ ☐ ☐ ☐ ☐ ☐

INGREDIENTS

_____ _____   _____ _____

_____ _____   _____ _____

_____ _____   _____ _____

_____ _____   _____ _____

GARNISH

INSTRUCTIONS

DIFFICULTY ○○○○○   OVERALL RATING ☆☆☆☆☆

GLASS TYPE

☐ ☐ ☐ ☐ ☐ ☐ ☐ ☐ ☐ ☐

INGREDIENTS

_____ _____   _____ _____

_____ _____   _____ _____

_____ _____   _____ _____

_____ _____   _____ _____

GARNISH

_____   _____

_____   _____

_____

INSTRUCTIONS

_____

_____

_____

_____

_____

_____

DIFFICULTY ○○○○○   **OVERALL RATING** ☆☆☆☆☆

NAME _____   DATE _____

GLASS TYPE

☐ ☐ ☐ ☐ ☐ ☐ ☐ ☐ ☐ ☐

INGREDIENTS

_____ _____   _____ _____

_____ _____   _____ _____

_____ _____   _____ _____

_____ _____   _____ _____

GARNISH

_____   _____

_____   _____

_____   _____

INSTRUCTIONS

_____

_____

_____

_____

_____

_____

DIFFICULTY ○○○○○   OVERALL RATING ☆☆☆☆☆

NAME ____________________ DATE ____________________

GLASS TYPE

☐ ☐ ☐ ☐ ☐ ☐ ☐ ☐ ☐ ☐

INGREDIENTS

GARNISH

INSTRUCTIONS

DIFFICULTY ○○○○○ OVERALL RATING ☆☆☆☆☆

🍸 NAME _____   📅 DATE _____

GLASS TYPE

☐ ☐ ☐ ☐ ☐ ☐ ☐ ☐ ☐ ☐

INGREDIENTS

_____ _____   _____ _____
_____ _____   _____ _____
_____ _____   _____ _____
_____ _____   _____ _____

GARNISH

_____   _____
_____   _____
_____   _____

INSTRUCTIONS

_____
_____
_____
_____
_____
_____

DIFFICULTY ○○○○○   OVERALL RATING ☆☆☆☆☆

NAME _____   📅 DATE _____

GLASS TYPE

☐ ☐ ☐ ☐ ☐ ☐ ☐ ☐ ☐ ☐

INGREDIENTS

_____ _____   _____ _____

_____ _____   _____ _____

_____ _____   _____ _____

_____ _____   _____ _____

GARNISH

_____   _____

_____   _____

_____   _____

INSTRUCTIONS

_____

_____

_____

_____

_____

_____

DIFFICULTY ○○○○○   OVERALL RATING ☆☆☆☆☆

NAME _____   DATE _____

GLASS TYPE

☐   ☐   ☐   ☐   ☐   ☐   ☐   ☐   ☐   ☐

INGREDIENTS

_____ _____ _____ _____

_____ _____ _____ _____

_____ _____ _____ _____

_____ _____ _____ _____

GARNISH

_____ _____

_____ _____

_____ _____

INSTRUCTIONS

_____

_____

_____

_____

_____

_____

DIFFICULTY ○○○○○   OVERALL RATING ☆☆☆☆☆

GLASS TYPE

☐ ☐ ☐ ☐ ☐ ☐ ☐ ☐ ☐ ☐

INGREDIENTS

_____ _____   _____ _____

_____ _____   _____ _____

_____ _____   _____ _____

_____ _____   _____ _____

GARNISH

_____   _____

_____   _____

_____   _____

INSTRUCTIONS

_____

_____

_____

_____

_____

DIFFICULTY ○○○○○   OVERALL RATING ☆☆☆☆☆

🍸 NAME _____   📅 DATE _____

GLASS TYPE

☐ ☐ ☐ ☐ ☐ ☐ ☐ ☐ ☐ ☐

INGREDIENTS

_____ _____   _____ _____

_____ _____   _____ _____

_____ _____   _____ _____

_____ _____   _____ _____

GARNISH

_____   _____

_____   _____

_____   _____

INSTRUCTIONS

_____

_____

_____

_____

_____

DIFFICULTY ○○○○○   OVERALL RATING ☆☆☆☆☆

🍸 NAME _____   📅 DATE _____

GLASS TYPE

☐ ☐ ☐ ☐ ☐ ☐ ☐ ☐ ☐ ☐

INGREDIENTS

_____ _____   _____ _____

_____ _____   _____ _____

_____ _____   _____ _____

_____ _____   _____ _____

GARNISH

_____   _____

_____   _____

_____   _____

INSTRUCTIONS

_____

_____

_____

_____

_____

DIFFICULTY ○○○○○   OVERALL RATING ☆☆☆☆☆

🍸 NAME _____   📅 DATE _____

GLASS TYPE

☐ ☐ ☐ ☐ ☐ ☐ ☐ ☐ ☐ ☐

INGREDIENTS

_____ _____   _____ _____
_____ _____   _____ _____
_____ _____   _____ _____
_____ _____   _____ _____

GARNISH

_____   _____
_____   _____
_____   _____

INSTRUCTIONS

_____
_____
_____
_____
_____

DIFFICULTY ○○○○○   OVERALL RATING ☆☆☆☆☆

GLASS TYPE

☐ ☐ ☐ ☐ ☐ ☐ ☐ ☐ ☐ ☐

INGREDIENTS

_____ _____   _____ _____

_____ _____   _____ _____

_____ _____   _____ _____

_____ _____   _____ _____

GARNISH

_____   _____

_____   _____

_____   _____

INSTRUCTIONS

_____

_____

_____

_____

_____

DIFFICULTY ○○○○○   OVERALL RATING ☆☆☆☆☆

GLASS TYPE

☐ ☐ ☐ ☐ ☐ ☐ ☐ ☐ ☐ ☐

INGREDIENTS

_____ _____   _____ _____

_____ _____   _____ _____

_____ _____   _____ _____

_____ _____   _____ _____

GARNISH

_____   _____

_____   _____

_____   _____

INSTRUCTIONS

_____

_____

_____

_____

_____

DIFFICULTY ⭘⭘⭘⭘⭘   OVERALL RATING ☆☆☆☆☆

🍸 NAME _____   📅 DATE _____

GLASS TYPE

☐ ☐ ☐ ☐ ☐ ☐ ☐ ☐ ☐ ☐

INGREDIENTS

_____ _____ _____ _____

_____ _____ _____ _____

_____ _____ _____ _____

_____ _____ _____ _____

GARNISH

_____ _____

_____ _____

_____ _____

INSTRUCTIONS

_____

_____

_____

_____

_____

_____

DIFFICULTY ○○○○○   OVERALL RATING ☆☆☆☆☆

GLASS TYPE

☐ ☐ ☐ ☐ ☐ ☐ ☐ ☐ ☐ ☐

INGREDIENTS

_____ _____   _____ _____

_____ _____   _____ _____

_____ _____   _____ _____

_____ _____   _____ _____

GARNISH

_____   _____

_____   _____

_____   _____

INSTRUCTIONS

_____

_____

_____

_____

_____

DIFFICULTY ○○○○○   OVERALL RATING ☆☆☆☆☆

NAME _____   DATE _____

GLASS TYPE

☐ ☐ ☐ ☐ ☐ ☐ ☐ ☐ ☐ ☐

INGREDIENTS

_____ _____   _____ _____

_____ _____   _____ _____

_____ _____   _____ _____

_____ _____   _____ _____

GARNISH

_____   _____

_____   _____

_____   _____

INSTRUCTIONS

_____

_____

_____

_____

_____

DIFFICULTY ○○○○○   OVERALL RATING ☆☆☆☆☆

GLASS TYPE

☐ ☐ ☐ ☐ ☐ ☐ ☐ ☐ ☐ ☐

INGREDIENTS

_____ _____   _____ _____

_____ _____   _____ _____

_____ _____   _____ _____

_____ _____   _____ _____

GARNISH

_____   _____

_____   _____

_____   _____

INSTRUCTIONS

_____

_____

_____

_____

_____

_____

DIFFICULTY ○○○○○   OVERALL RATING ☆☆☆☆☆

🍸 NAME _____   📅 DATE _____

GLASS TYPE

☐ ☐ ☐ ☐ ☐ ☐ ☐ ☐ ☐ ☐

INGREDIENTS

_____ _____   _____ _____

_____ _____   _____ _____

_____ _____   _____ _____

_____ _____   _____ _____

GARNISH

_____   _____

_____   _____

_____   _____

INSTRUCTIONS

_____

_____

_____

_____

_____

DIFFICULTY ○○○○○   OVERALL RATING ☆☆☆☆☆

NAME _____   DATE _____

GLASS TYPE

☐ ☐ ☐ ☐ ☐ ☐ ☐ ☐ ☐ ☐

INGREDIENTS

_____ _____   _____ _____

_____ _____   _____ _____

_____ _____   _____ _____

_____ _____   _____ _____

GARNISH

_____   _____

_____   _____

_____   _____

INSTRUCTIONS

_____

_____

_____

_____

_____

DIFFICULTY ○○○○○   OVERALL RATING ☆☆☆☆☆

🍸 NAME _____   📅 DATE _____

GLASS TYPE

☐ ☐ ☐ ☐ ☐ ☐ ☐ ☐ ☐ ☐

INGREDIENTS

_____ _____   _____ _____

_____ _____   _____ _____

_____ _____   _____ _____

_____ _____   _____ _____

GARNISH

_____   _____

_____   _____

_____   _____

INSTRUCTIONS

_____

_____

_____

_____

_____

DIFFICULTY ○○○○○   OVERALL RATING ☆☆☆☆☆

NAME _____   ## DATE _____

GLASS TYPE

☐ ☐ ☐ ☐ ☐ ☐ ☐ ☐ ☐ ☐

INGREDIENTS

_____ _____   _____ _____

_____ _____   _____ _____

_____ _____   _____ _____

_____ _____   _____ _____

GARNISH

_____   _____

_____   _____

_____   _____

INSTRUCTIONS

_____

_____

_____

_____

_____

DIFFICULTY ○○○○○   OVERALL RATING ☆☆☆☆☆

🍸 NAME _____   📅 DATE _____

GLASS TYPE

☐ ☐ ☐ ☐ ☐ ☐ ☐ ☐ ☐ ☐

INGREDIENTS

_____ _____   _____ _____

_____ _____   _____ _____

_____ _____   _____ _____

_____ _____   _____ _____

GARNISH

_____   _____

_____   _____

_____   _____

INSTRUCTIONS

_____

_____

_____

_____

_____

DIFFICULTY ⭘⭘⭘⭘⭘   OVERALL RATING ☆☆☆☆☆

NAME _____   DATE _____

GLASS TYPE

☐ ☐ ☐ ☐ ☐ ☐ ☐ ☐ ☐ ☐

INGREDIENTS

_____ _____   _____ _____

_____ _____   _____ _____

_____ _____   _____ _____

_____ _____   _____ _____

GARNISH

_____   _____

_____   _____

_____   _____

INSTRUCTIONS

_____

_____

_____

_____

_____

_____

DIFFICULTY ○○○○○   OVERALL RATING ☆☆☆☆☆

NAME _____   DATE _____

GLASS TYPE

☐ ☐ ☐ ☐ ☐ ☐ ☐ ☐ ☐ ☐

INGREDIENTS

_____ _____   _____ _____

_____ _____   _____ _____

_____ _____   _____ _____

_____ _____   _____ _____

GARNISH

_____   _____

_____   _____

_____   _____

INSTRUCTIONS

_____

_____

_____

_____

_____

_____

DIFFICULTY ○○○○○   OVERALL RATING ☆☆☆☆☆

Cocktail Recipe Ideas

- ○ _____
- ○ _____
- ○ _____
- ○ _____
- ○ _____
- ○ _____
- ○ _____
- ○ _____
- ○ _____
- ○ _____
- ○ _____
- ○ _____
- ○ _____
- ○ _____
- ○ _____
- ○ _____
- ○ _____
- ○ _____
- ○ _____
- ○ _____
- ○ _____
- ○ _____
- ○ _____

- ○ _____
- ○ _____
- ○ _____
- ○ _____
- ○ _____
- ○ _____
- ○ _____
- ○ _____
- ○ _____
- ○ _____
- ○ _____
- ○ _____
- ○ _____
- ○ _____
- ○ _____
- ○ _____
- ○ _____
- ○ _____
- ○ _____
- ○ _____
- ○ _____
- ○ _____
- ○ _____

Cocktail Recipe Ideas

○ _____	○ _____
○ _____	○ _____
○ _____	○ _____
○ _____	○ _____
○ _____	○ _____
○ _____	○ _____
○ _____	○ _____
○ _____	○ _____
○ _____	○ _____
○ _____	○ _____
○ _____	○ _____
○ _____	○ _____
○ _____	○ _____
○ _____	○ _____
○ _____	○ _____
○ _____	○ _____
○ _____	○ _____
○ _____	○ _____
○ _____	○ _____
○ _____	○ _____
○ _____	○ _____
○ _____	○ _____
○ _____	○ _____
○ _____	○ _____

NOTES

NOTES

THANK YOU

IF YOU ENJOYED THIS BOOK
PLEASE CONSIDER LEAVING A RATING
AND HELP US WITH YOUR
BRIEF AND HONEST REVIEW.

IT REALLY MEANS A LOT TO US!